Lullaby (with Exit Sign)

Hadara Bar-Nadav

saturnalia books

Distributed by University Press of New England
Hanover and London

Saturnalia Books
105 Woodside Rd.
Ardmore, PA 19003
info@saturnaliabooks.com

ISBN: 978-0-9833686-6-3
Library of Congress Control Number: 2012920639

Book Design by Saturnalia Books
Printing by Westcan Printing Group, Canada

Cover Art: Allison Schulnik, *Skipping Skeletons,* 2008. Oil on canvas, 84" x 136", Collection: Nerman Museum of Contemporary Art, Johnson County Community College, Overland Park, Kansas. Gift of Marti and Tony Oppenheimer, Los Angeles, California.

Cover Design: Richard Every

Distributed by:
University Press of New England
1 Court Street
Lebanon, NH 03766
800-421-1561

Grateful acknowledgment is made to the editors of the following publications in which these poems or versions of these poems first appeared: *Agni, American Letters & Commentary, American Poetry Review, Barrow Street, Bellingham Review, Beloit Poetry Journal, The Cincinnati Review, The Colorado Review, Court Green, Crazyhorse, Denver Quarterly, Hotel Amerika, Jet Fuel Review, The Journal, New American Writing, Parcel, Ploughshares, POOL, Prairie Schooner, Sentence,* and *TriQuarterly.*

With endless thanks to Lynn Emanuel for selecting this book for the Saturnalia Books Poetry Prize and to Henry Israeli and the wonderful staff of Saturnalia Books. With thanks to Simone Muench for her great spirit and fierce editorial eye. Thanks also to Kevin Prufer for his boundless generosity, warmth, and poetic vision. To Wayne Miller, Rebecca Morgan Frank, Cyrus Console, and Jake Adam York for their friendship and astute editorial insights. To my colleagues and students at the University of Missouri-Kansas City. To the Vermont Studio Center and the Virginia Center for the Creative Arts, where some of these poems were born. And to Scott George Beattie, my light.

For my family

In memory of Moty Simcha Bar-Nadav

and of V

Contents

Good-bye—the Going utter me—
Goodnight, I still reply

—Emily Dickinson

Lullaby (with Exit Sign)

I slept with all four hooves
> in the air or I slept like a snail

> in my broken shell.

The periphery of the world
> dissolved. A giant exit sign

> blinking above my head.

My family sings
> its death march.

> They are the size of the moon.

No, they are the size
> of thumbtacks punched

> through the sky's eyelid.

What beauty, what bruise.

(What strange lullaby is this

that sings from its wound?)

Here, my dead father knocks

on a little paper door. Here

my family knocks, waits.

Come through me, my darlings

whatever you are: flame,

lampshade, soap.

Leave your shattered shadows

behind. I'll be the doorway

that watches you go.

I.

Compose an Evening Sky

that resists. Neon-lit with greasy oranges and pinks. Funereal flowers weep entire, damp with wilting. Clutch a tourist's postcard of the slivered night (which means we're just visiting). *Father, I am poor once more* without you. This bloody weather rubs me thin. Thin breath. Skinned ribs. Snow geese cry overhead, a proscenium of crumple and din. The phosphorescent scar of the moon turns its pocked cheek.

Now descends a blackened-blue scrim clotted with lint. A molting of just moments before. Azure decomposure. Erosion's humble fate. This edgeless blankery poor without you. Your palace nightly disintegrates.

I Dreaded that First Robin, So

That willful singing. Blare of arrival and ache of thaw. My hands stinging with bloodheat. I preferred fingers of ice fringing the windows and doors. Fringes made pear-yellow in the sun, so the world is tinted distant-soft. The roads untouched. The grass asleep. No note rippling the landscape. Mind filling with wind. A timeless now—a pause here that resists spin. *I dared not meet the Daffodils.* Those bile-yellow skirts shock the eyes from reverie. All morning, the robin's rust-red cry, too eager for its season. Relentless trumpet, trumpet, twitter. Face of a trollop, voice like tin. This garish onslaught of spring.

I Don't Like Paradise

though the candy is nice and all things broken are whole again. Father unpins his raveled limbs, repairs the impairment of paralysis and blot of stroke. The clot now eased, the blood released, wanders the heart, humming. And there is mother's puzzled face. The maze of surgical welts dissolves. Melanomic swirls like cinnamon melt. Our juicy mouths gloss sweet. We are sugary plastic, a shiny Paradise. But *I never felt at Home* in shiny. Felt the starlings darkly underskin, their mustard points beaking through the taffy chew of us. Our bitter cup of collapse. If they scavenge the too-small opening of our ears or devour our eyes, a thousand wings will sour the scene, and all things broken break again.

Split the Lark

The lock. The dark. The eyes of a man who loved birds. Let's step outside, try a *Scarlet Experiment* in the afternoon. At first you see nothing, a brilliant heat. Sharp seam of spring where sorrow meets song. Tender turns to tenderize. Turn skyward, mouth like a church. Where does the whistle live? Little god you open, search. Knife-red feather in the twine of the lemon tree. A leather-throated cry and your eyes pinch closed. Sequins wink along the lining of the lids. The sky like a ball gown, ball-gown grass, ball-gown stop sign. The taffeta dog. Everywhere lavender suns, diamonds of bloodless light. Memory remembers you seeing. Still, the eyes are blind.

Prayer Is the Little Implement

Tool or tooth. Carving or cut. Lesion lined in mud. In this way, words are not accretion, like rain where the gatherings glimmer and fall. Fail. And fail a word for the body giving out, as in: your father is failing. Prayers gather and fall. Fail. *No other Art would do.* If this is art, puddle and swell, so the garden eventually drowns. Each grain, each letter, another meager little. Defenseless tool in a deluge. Eyelash to row your boat. Sing a song to keep us company while we soak through: Little Woe Weep has lost her sleep, or a hack on pills went up a hill to fetch a pain of daughter. Put down the scalpel and syntax. The meaningless hum of rain.

Family of Strangers

Ghosts multiply, spreading
      while I sleep.

Ghosts born two at a time, tearing
from my nostrils, and a large child
who bubbles from my mouth and suckles my chin.

Once-black eyes now alive
with iridescent fog.

      Blue electricity needles.

Some ghosts are children who stare
at me while I sleep.

Some are fathers who can walk again,
smoke streaming from their hair.

      In daylight I miss you.

I begin to miss you when
I am peeling from sleep, edges
reddening with sun.

Ghosts, I adore your absence.

Ghosts, I cannot lie to you
who are transparent, I
who am also transparent.

In daylight I pretend to stop
loving, to stop looking for you,
ghost children, ghost men—

Let us never be absent or calm.

The Angle of a Landscape

Blackbirds pluck the trees, throat bloody notes through limbs and eaves. Such radiant violence. The sky, a nacred sheet. The *Forehead of a hill* cracked open so the ghosts rip free. A height once whole, a peak from which to see. Between the curtain and the wall rusts the world through a window. A nest with four teal eggs, dotted gray. Yolk and plaster, pastel-caked. Here, blackbird. Here, landscape. To watch your watching without recognition, without name. Grass-line, tree-line, hairline breaks in the glass, the gauze, the gaze. Your head wanders, nodding like a cradle.

Run Round and Round a Room

The head like an oubliette. Forget. Forget. How to escape your medieval form? Shave the scalp, chisel and drill. Excise a square of skull. Pain awaits when you wake. *Obscure with Fog* and pills. Nervous and nervouser. We have loved too long. Believed in words and spheres. Scalpels make a paper cut-out of your former self, silhouette stitched to wind. Let them scour the edge, search the unguent inch while you radiate, glow from within. Let them ogle the permutation: a doorway where a man once lived.

Dust Is the Only Secret

Tender father. Feather your face. Fingers laced with June. This waiting room white as always. July. You were patient. August. Body of wilted springs. Part tissue. Part decay. Paralysis. September, and the months drip. Patience. Pain. *Infinite contain.* Patient between 3 a.m. and Tuesday. Between sponge bath and morphine. Between warfarin and vomiting. Current, rubber, hiccup, vex. The body lit up, needled, electric. You dream, half-life, half-lit. Machines chirp metallic lullabies. A neon line blinks across a black screen. Pulse like a promise *green* and *green* until the heart stops, sleeps.

I Sing to Use the Waiting

in the nervous room, in the white room with nervous hands. Every *Hour is a Sea* swallowing me. The loudspeaker sputters, mumbling to the air like a drunk. Two children take turns screaming from either side of the room (or I am the children screaming from my mouth to my ears). A man in white finally appears. He explains things, expresses condolences without expressing a thing, talks with steady hands, palms up, to show rehearsed sympathies. He is full of meaning and walks away. Goodbye meaning in your white coat. Now the waiting will never end.

Infection in the Sentence Breeds

Taste of tin and hiccup of blood. The mouth flaps open, floods—. A Rorschach of roses surprisingly red: reddest, full of throat. In this terrible sea wish for a boat. Slipperiness sets into stain, nibbles the sheets. Tongue-prints the size of fists. *A Word dropped*, choked. With commas come a promise, with dashes come piece—misshapen grammar writ in bone.

I overhear an orderly say he breaks the limbs too stiff to fold. I *over* hear, I hear the plastered glint of hospital white, the tongue's needle-high song. Staples stitch my mouth, the jaw pinched closed.

Blind Fragment

They wore strange faces.

No, they were nurses

spun in gauze dresses,

shadows of their legs

beneath, and another

(buttonless) who held

my wrist and nodded,

but touch is touch

full of feeling and skin

so I thought

I recognized each

of them *hello*, *hello*,

so none of us was alone

as my bowels groaned

and I slipped through

my mouth, beyond

the window outside,

and clung to a cypress,

its funnel of green,

so I could watch us

a little while more,

but the drift in the wind

was warm, a yawn

pulling me upward

on strings.

II.

Donor (Wind)

The throat is optional,

as is the larynx.

What small object

can you pull

through the pink?

Many things died here:

a nest, an oil leak,

a typewriter ribbon's

language of bile

and thread. Spread

my useless parts

in the city dump,

spleen fondled by

seagulls, vertebrae

plucked by lonely men.

Tape my useless

parts together again

and I'm your dis

-appearing shatter.

Your snowflake

in heat. Now feed

me to the wind

where I belong.

Upon the Slowest Night

To keep the soul company, seethe and pray, and the prayer must be constant so the dead can find his way. Every hour the watcher shifts, so the soul is not alone in this room of closed eyes and damp vowels. When I enter, the walls curl inward, cornering me. His unadorned form draped in a single white sheet. The seconds crush: *Grief is Tongueless*. Do not leave. Do not leave me alone. Broke of syntax. Quit of speech. The soul drifting, already in transit.

From Blank to Blank

A body in a room. No room inside the body. Untenable nouns. Untenable fount of the mouth. Here you were breathing. Here you are not. *A Presence of Departed Acts.*

From the room where I waited to a waiting room to a room where waiting ended. That hollowed space whispered full of pleases, groping like hands. Corridor. Corridor. Door and daylight. Gravity bearing down like glass. I walk behind myself—dragging, detached. All is airless aftermath.

To Bear on Us Unshaded

We bow our heads and burn. Heat scalding the back of our necks, singeing our crowns. The sun opens over us. The sun wants to burn us into the ground. Scent of soil, glittering, cloying, sick with goodbyes. We swelter, wither, prayer stuck in our parched mouths. Birds descend, *declaim their Tunes*—piercing us with bright cries. Cardinals streak the day with blood. We follow our sad shadows, swallow our tongues. We are done. We are done. We are done.

Let Us Chant It Softly

Let the man in velvet be velvet. *Let me not mar that perfect Dream.* Let the words not be particulate and full of bite. Let the worms not feast. Let the oily slip of their flesh know salt. Let the salt know each of their names. Let their rigorous muscles rigorously unthread. Let each of their coils wring each of their necks. Let suffocation be slow. Let their kingdom stop churning, let their kingdom be still. And my father whole again.

The Afterlife of Dust

Now you are slipping into the deafening dirt
        and the sparrows have taken note.

That childhood song about potatoes
        where you mixed up the numbers and the hands . . . .

Make a list of happinesses to remember you by.
        Line the eyelids inside.

Make memory bright the projection-screen.
        Add butter, add picturesque.

Thank the dark for its tireless shine
        and Technicolored manipulation.

Now I can make you whatever I want.
        Sit down at my table and become.

What Care the Dead for Day

who linger, who watch as I once did from the high corner of a dream, floating above your hospital bed. I attended night for you. *I guarded my Master's Head*. In dreams I gave you eyes. I gave you a shiny network of veins and a stopless heart. New forms to carry you, bind you to the day. I should have wished your body away—erased the flesh of you, the flaw.

The World Is Not Conclusion

Answers the size of silence. Tall as tidal winds. The fracture of letters and numbers pulled like wool up to my chin. Grid the knowable world from the sweat of my bed. An empty set. Count the seasons, count the sheep, count the dead. If word equaled father equaled alive again. If morning equaled apple equaled sated, sweet. Equations misfire, undaughter me. Try to forward the mind, distract with babble, equivocate. *A Questioning dissolves.* Solves no ache.

And Leaves the Shreds Behind

Shards. A sharp congress of ghosts. A flurry of ink-dark wings, hectic clouds. This grief you cannot swallow. Memory winces, rasps you to twig. The afterbite of death whittles. Whips. Father sky, father soil, father rain. He has *littered all the East.* He is everywhere. Omniscient wind. Lead-black horizon, lightning veined. Though you huddle, tremble, pray for sleep, his wild calligraphy cuts the trees. Riddled skies claim you.

Close Your Eyes to Catch a Ghost

I carry my dead
        under my eyelids

            who yawn and pull out

my stitches, who yawn
        and sing to my teeth.

            One night of shivering,

another of sweat. They beat
        my ear canals like bells

            and whisper along the length

of my neck. One chanting
        Hebrew cries out: 1/8 and 2/3,

            and this is an alphabet,

a blessing in language
        deranged by shadows

            and wings. Goodnight, I reply,

though I am alone and they
        are full of tricks. I forgive

            the dead and let them reign—

now that they are dead
        they will never know sleep.

III.

Lamb

My family destroys the lamb.
The lamb destroys my family.

I pass out, hoofed child,
on your moist, hot back.

You softly count the knives.
You sharpen each with your bleat.

You continue bleating until
my ears cry. Make it stop.

Make it stop, my sweet lamb.
I need you. Otherwise, hunger

would mince my shriveled heart.
You wouldn't run away

with your warm thighs
wrapped in lovely white curls.

You are a work of art,
an orchestra, a church.

God knows the tender
meat of your hocks,

your pink mouth, lashes
like a young girl's curling

over black eyes that look
at me without recognition,

without a blood thought.
I am seized by the young

daughter I lost. I am grass.
Grief. The oven opening

wide as you drift to sleep.

One Need Not Be a House

Each doorway warping. Each window sprung. The living room with its singing nails, the chimney with its crumbling mouth of ash. Who sits in the chairs, who sighs on the porch, who collects dust on her tongue, waiting? Whose dress is a shadow the curtain makes? Say it plainly: To be alive is *to be Haunted*; to be dead is to haunt. Who calls your name? We do. Who speaks from your mouth? We do. Father, mother, daughter, we do. A seat for you at our table.

Ruin Is Formal

Glassware (skin). Silverware (stitch). A crepe-thin blanket and your body disembodied beneath. A white picnic. And you slowly rousing, strangely light, singular from this other sleep. Blowsy drips of iodine. *Elemental Rust* streaking your cheek. You recall a girl's name from your life before: Fannie (fentanyl). Lori, Pam (lorazepam). A girlhood ago. Girl in a gown. A dressing. Cast. Someone wound in clinical linen. Pupa. Spider's catch. White ribbons a woman might wear to hide the weeping wound of her face. A hole where absence pools. Lakes. Her lost eye in a somewhere sea, seeing nothing.

Darkness Intersects Her Face

To look at her was to see a fire, skin pulling away from skin, cancer blistering its meat. The surgeon had been thorough, neat. She wore her thigh on her cheek, her neck on her forehead, her eyelid cut from her inner arm. And so it seemed she was all crust and seam, more marionette than mother. More wire than whole. *Behind this mortal Bone*, a shadow is growing inside her. No, love is growing inside her, touching every part.

A Little Madness in the Spring

An orgy of insects vibrates and rubs, sexing the light. A haze of wires and wings, insistent little clocks. If I smash the buzzing gears with my hand, if I wear my own blood, can I then stop, step out of time? This threat of days, thrust of decay. A grassling splits open rock. Everyone loves this *whole Experiment of Green*. I don't. The dead disintegrate underground, the living disintegrate above. What dread, this virulent season. Viridian spring twitches and multiplies, metastasizes, flashes her cellular smirk.

Each Scar I'll Keep for Him

who made me. My blind god who carved the facets of my face. He fated
me for this: grafts etched in silver, in waxy pink. A kaleidoscope of pain
fractures my eye, shatters through the bell of my brain, and this means a
nerve is reborn. Awakening in pieces, piecemeal, remembering each line
contains its own glimmering.

My wounds are public, an elaborate display dressed in amber gauze, black
stitchery, or translucent yellow beaded with glue. I will not look, not look
away. Each person who beholds my face *Holds a Sun on Me*. Diamond-
bright, blinding.

To Ache Is Human

Nerves that needle, riddle, stab, and itch. Damaged nerves, deranged nerves, nerves furiously ticking, ticking. The nerve in nervous, in sever and serve. *If your Nerve deny you*, punish it, coddle it, signal its demise. Nerves recoil before a nerve strike. Nerve bark or bite. Nerve spindle, spider, electromagnetic splay. Nerves aflame like a chandelier branching across the ceiling of the day. Radiating nerves, a picture in writhe, in red. A sunrise without beauty.

Suspension

I will mar, will mark
the surface. Strike
black and gold.

> How much bone
> do you need to
> recognize my face?

There were photos
for the reconstruction,
the way I used to be.

> A bridge wrapped
> in skin. You could say
> a beige masterpiece.

Effortless nose, effortless
pupils that read the light,
excellent muscled eggs.

> And now the yank
> of scaffolding, cosmetic
> pink for fissures,

rouge for lips. My open-
casket mouth packed
with putty. Fixed.

Lift the Flesh Door

Begin at the divot of the neck and pull up, over chin, nose, the wasted eyes; the eyes where sequins lived. Slip off the scalp, each hair trembling once before it gives. Peel back the ears, small shells of blood and listening. Unhood the whole head; the head now free. Release shoulders, wrists, the blue lacework of veins. Unhook each rib, toss vertebrae to wind. The waist flaps open, expands, drifts. The liver tumbles out, slippery, steaming, fat as a piglet. Peel, pull, the job's almost done. Unzip genitals, pelvis, the oval bowl of the hips. Dismantle the legs, knees, toes. Internal pillars, scaffolding of bone. Empty. Breathe. Formless. Rest. *Lean against the Grave* you were. Soul picked clean of self.

We Cover Thee—Sweet Face—

We blanket, locket, keepsake. We daguerreotype and velvet case. We boutonniere and casket. We bury you in a desert, bless you in a foreign alphabet. We dress you in a flag, slip you out to sea. We burn you free of body, empty your remains under a cypress tree. We ash and urn memory, rearrange your final shape. A version of you always with us *Sequestered from Decay.*

The One Who Could Repeat a Summer Day

who skipped rope and the whip of time was yellow with fumble and fear. A fitful here. If I thought too hard, I missed. Misstepped. Steeped in sightless sun. Better buttercups. Better jam. And the starlings I loved with their spoon-small heads. Soon I was not thinking. Flutter instead. *The Feet, mechanical, go round.* Mathematics of rhythm at bay. The legs know how to walk without the head. My father with an axe and the chickens blind with running, red. A headless dance for whole minutes. Minus their names: Linus. Micky. Abigail. Thought gets in the way. Thought gives way. The body's involuntary twitching.

How Soft This Prison Is

Body, bundle, country of twigs. Your nine gates opening, closing, spittle wet. A miracle you existed at all. Fontanel, fallible. Your soul shaking inside. When you died, *Leaves unhooked themselves from Trees*. I watched them go like little mouths, dried and paper-flat, without music. Ticker tape in shades of blood-orange, rust. And the wind did gently lay you down. I waited. I watched.

Ample as the Eye

is not. I see you in the mirror, nailhead, godhead. A shine so black. A task so small. Focus the dark. Do I expand, flexing for light? But am not conscious of it, this opening, closing. How like breath you are, forgotten. The brain says look and you do, you become a window, refuse to turn away. See the ruined farmhouse made of moths and broken limbs, the ruined frame through which the world is failing. *In my Chamber*, the dark turns red, shadows lit by burning. Red glass, red moon, lashes rimmed in blood. A bath of heat and wakefulness.

Rabbit (Rapid)

White tuft, magnetic prey. Night
           rippling through blood, eyes.

I will never feel safe, small
           as a cup, so that I can stop

trembling: hair, lungs, puddle
           of sky. You see me, whetting

the green of my spring.
           You inhale me like a whisper

in a closet of coats. My face
           blackens with shadows and I see

how the night was born.
           You step your white-footed step

away from me. I smell you:
           fear, fur, musk. Around us

vinyl siding sinks. An old Buick
           wheezes by helpless as the gingko,

azalea, telephone pole. I stand
           in humming grass, a mosquito

feast around my feet, and shiver
           in the night in which you shiver,

our garden of rain and blood.

IV.

Palace

When they run out of meat

         men disappear. I chew
    my hair, a kind of fullness

that is kind, a thread

         soup. A nest gathers
    its strands inside me.

The dead hatch, translucent-eyed,

         wire-boned, small
    whistling through beaks.

We share our (secret)

         feast, miles of hair to keep
    us warm. I rock

on my heels in the middle

         of the day and lull
    their yellow points to sleep.

I smile at the humming

fences. I smile when men shave
me down and number me.

I become succulent, round.

My nipples, a bright pink.
Like a little cat I lick

the hair from my arms, tongue

salt from my hands.
We make a fat

oven of us, a place beyond

hunger, beyond melt
and match. The birds flap

full-grown, ash-black—

hundreds rise from
my palace of ribs.

I Would Have Starved a Gnat

This lean of bone and tilt. All odd angles to the sun. Flut. Flet. Flatten me
with your mad flit. Your fast tying hands. All odd angles and eminent
collapse. Now on our knees. Now bowing. Please, kiss my littlest one. A
video found in a bunker underground. I once was a night. Once nightly
news. See the vultures and gnats flock to our shivering. *Food's necessity*
Upon me—like a Claw—. A gathering of wingly things so all you see is
weather. Turning iridescent. Turning black. The kingdom of the body
blown to ash. Buttons of us left in the sun. The crown and the teeth. The
aftermath. No moist benevolent thing between us. Take me. Take half.

The Hour of Lead

fed me the leveling terror of tar. Liquid supped through a tube. No, liquid floods, rushes, cools where it touches me everywhere, a glazed melt. All this electrical fanning, drowning from the inside. The Gods of Preservation penciled me in for Tuesday afternoon. Innards removed, plastic-packed. Neck and wrists veined with formaldehyde perfume. O, pickle my dead heart. Was I more than this forgettable vat of memory and fat, this container of flesh drunk on brine? *The letting go* was my entire life. I gorge and swell, still pinned to my spine. A chemical permanence blues my eyes.

Grief Is a Mouse

Now I am small, scratching the dark. A machine of bones and fur, nibbling the wall. Plaster and paint scrape the roof of my mouth. I *couldn't coax a syllable*. But something gives, breaks down, crown molding I push with my head. The dark presses me onward, will not rest. I chew through teeth, gums, and blood. Who knows what trap awaits—metal spring, black boot heel, fanged feline with moon-silver eyes. The dark licks its lips and lies: on the other side of the wall is a field, a green into which you can disappear.

Before We Say Goodbye

The tornado alarm sings

and sings. Women

with wind for hair.

Women with wind

in their mouths. Who

can sleep with all this

singing? The ghosts

are harmonic and

tear-filled. The ghosts

dash their heads on

the rocks. One dog

and then another begin.

One person's voice

climbs another until

we all are singing (blood

in the throat). All of us

singing and the sky

singing too. The sky

greening, glowing,

calls each of our names.

Death Is a Dialogue

in a long sleep so we speak in dreams, touching foreheads. You are feather and cry. I am fur and rust. *Necromancy Sweet.* I listen and you lead me to your home of dark where roots spine and ribbon the walls. Roots twin, trine, multiply. Giddy as children they tunnel and form new roadways, new houses you claim as your own. I ask then where is my home? When you point to your mouth, my ears ring.

A Brittle Heaven

ices over. Leafless. Listless. Heaven only an idea scraping out its breath.
Such cloudy disappearances. Pentimento, palimpsest. The fade of you still
lingers. Blue air splinters white. Was ever-after a wish, once upon a lie?
Here again I miss, I wake. *The Sky Ungained* by footfall. Morning cracks,
reseals itself in ice. Lacework scars the windows, scribbled maps derange the
light.

Then Draw My Little Letter Forth

Folded, pressed against my forehead. Scent of your tobaccoed hands. Hands the color of olive wood, fingertips yellow with years. Your letter hums in my night jacket, breast pocket, coat pocket. Daily I walk with you, wake with you daily. The dread of fraying corners and dust. I think of your hands thinking of me and *slowly pick the lock* on the day we will tear apart. When I open the page, your voice rises.

The Landscape Listens

Makes room for you in its grass bed. Here is the sun, yellow and round, small enough to fit in your pocket. And here's an oak tree you can balance on your thumb. Pigeon wings whistle overhead and the song is not crying. For a moment, death releases. Relents. The hill pillows, eyelids blanket. *Shadows hold their breath.* The easy alphabet of leaf and leaf, little rafts in a black season.

Master (Pieces)

—an erasure of Emily Dickinson's Master Letters

I.

        I am ill
though
        sweet

        I wish
        the Violets are
very near

I wish
I
could paint
disobedient
        messages

        The sun goes
down,
        Dawn
                again

Listen
I did not tell you
I cannot ~~talk~~
        pain
recollect[s]
        love.

II.

Who
bends her smaller life
                    to make
A love so big it
                    never flinched

but
sheltered him in her
                    (Heart)

            yet
                        she
grieved
her odd
            ~~troubled~~ sense

            teach her grace—
teach her majesty

            open her

Wonder
            wastes
                        my
brown eyes—
stabs
                        strains

when
dying
comes
I will   be
           your best little
           dear

III.

        If you saw a bullet
hit a
           word—
           would you believe
           in
God

           I didn't
           I don't

    ~~you had altered me~~
    ~~this stranger become~~
          ~~my breath~~

           I might
breathe where you breathed
and find
        night
           sorrow
                  frost
           love

I fear
        the Heart in
your breast

a timbrel is it
a tune
~~reverent~~
a syllable

Could you forget (me)

I used to think when I died
I could see you
                    Master

Could you come
                    Would you
        come

play in the woods—till
Dark

            till
I
[be]come

Bird   Ether

And with What Body Do They Come?

A dead man talks through my mouth. His guttural bass joins the high chatter of my grandmother and aunt whose words cough chimney smoke. Here comes the child I lost before she breathed and a man who trills the names of birds: star, star, starling, he chips his way through my teeth. Mother may I cut out my tongue. *The saddest noise, the sweetest noise.* Please, please, she keens.

I Read My Sentence

Unsentence it there. Pry the comma's hook. Lift with hammer's claw or thumbnail. Unloose the current of next and next. Shadows appear in their ink dress. Letterforms with arms like a girl: shoulder, leg, bowl, stem flailing in a white sea. Dash table, dash pen, dash raft. Each mark too small to carry breath. What becomes us: marginalia. You once were. Then. Letters through which a promise drifts, until *the Matter ends*.

The Lungs Are Stirless

Starless. Those little pearls of breath lining the walls, once heaving, lit. And now they've gone to seed. Now the children are dead. Each ago. Each then. Each with its own delicate shade: linen, bone, cloud, yellow-glazed. Each with its own ruffled neck. *Saying itself in new inflection,* I was one of those children. Death came fast. Or it didn't. No one was spared. We left our wasted home and walked into the world across a woman's lips.

Notes

Italicized titles and italicized phrases within these poems are adapted from Emily Dickinson's poetry. I am indebted to Dickinson and to *Final Harvest: Emily Dickinson's Poems*, selected and introduced by Thomas H. Johnson (Little, Brown and Company, 1961).

"Donor (Wind)" was inspired by Catie Rosemurgy's Miss Peach series of poems from *The Stranger Manual* (Graywolf Press, 2010).

"Lamb" was inspired by Tomaž Šalamun's poem "Spring Street" from *There's the Hand and There's the Arid Chair* (Counterpath Press, 2009).

"Master (Pieces)" is an erasure of Emily Dickinson's Master Letters as printed in *The Master Letters of Emily Dickinson*, edited by R.W. Franklin (Amherst College Press, 2002).

Also available from saturnalia books:

No Object by Natalie Shapero

Nowhere Fast by William Kulik

Arco Iris by Sarah Vap

The Girls of Peculiar by Catherine Pierce

Xing by Debora Kuan

Other Romes by Derek Mong

Faulkner's Rosary by Sarah Vap

Tsim Tsum by Sabrina Orah Mark

Hush Sessions by Kristi Maxwell

Days of Unwilling by Cal Bedient

Gurlesque: the new grrly, grotesque, burlesque poetics edited by Lara Glenum and
Arielle Greenberg

Letters to Poets: Conversations about Poetics, Politics, and Community
edited by Jennifer Firestone and Dana Teen Lomax

Artist/Poet Collaboration Series:
Velleity's Shade by Star Black / Artwork by Bill Knott
Polytheogamy by Timothy Liu / Artwork by Greg Drasler
Midnights by Jane Miller / Artwork by Beverly Pepper
Stigmata Errata Etcetera by Bill Knott / Artwork by Star Black
Ing Grish by John Yau / Artwork by Thomas Nozkowski
Blackboards by Tomaz Salamun / Artwork by Metka Krasovec

Previous Winners of the Saturnalia Books Poetry Prize:
My Scarlet Ways by Tanya Larkin
The Little Office of the Immaculate Conception by Martha Silano
Personification by Margaret Ronda
To the Bone by Sebastian Agudelo
Famous Last Words by Catherine Pierce
Dummy Fire by Sarah Vap
Correspondence by Kathleen Graber
The Babies by Sabrina Orah Mark

Lullaby (with Exit Sign) was printed using the font Adobe Garamond Pro.

www.saturnaliabooks.org